HYMNED

TABLE OF CONTENTS

TRANSCRIPTIONS & ENGRAVINGS BY LIVING STONE MUSIC CO. LLC

© 2005 INTEGRITY MEDIA, INC. 1000 CODY ROAD, MOBILE, AL 36695. ALL SONGS USED BY PERMISSION. ALL RIGHTS RESERVED. INTERNATIONAL RIGHTS SECURED. UNAUTHORIZED DUPLICATION IS A VIOLATION OF APPLICABLE LAWS. PRINTED IN THE U.S.A.

Just A Closer Walk With Thee

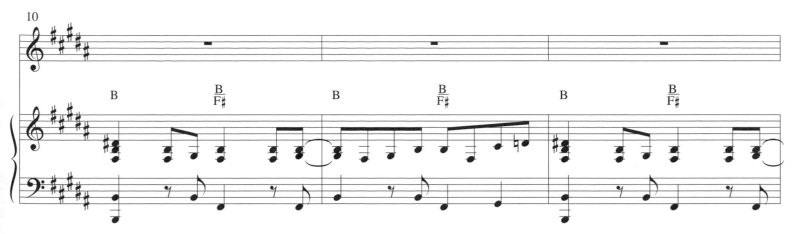

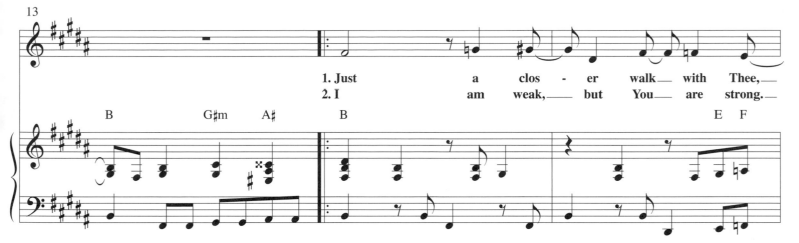

1. Just a clos - er walk with Thee,
2. I am weak, but You are strong.

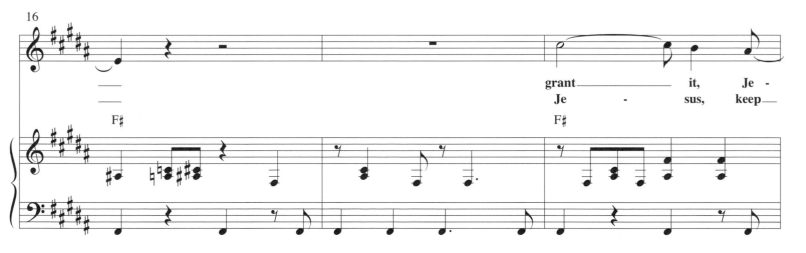

grant it, Je -
Je - sus, keep

- sus, is my plea.
me from all wrong.

Dai - ly___ walk - ing close___ to Thee,_____
I'll_____ be sat - is - fied___ as long_____

___ let it be,___ dear Lord,___ let it be.___
___ as I walk,___ let me walk close to Thee.___

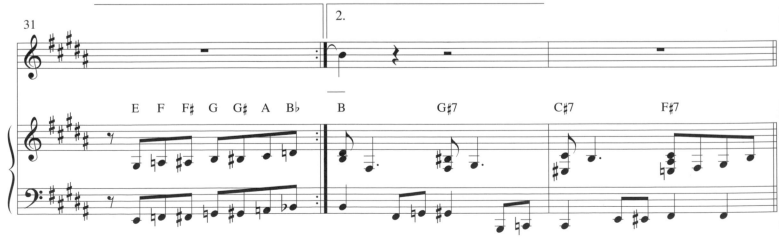

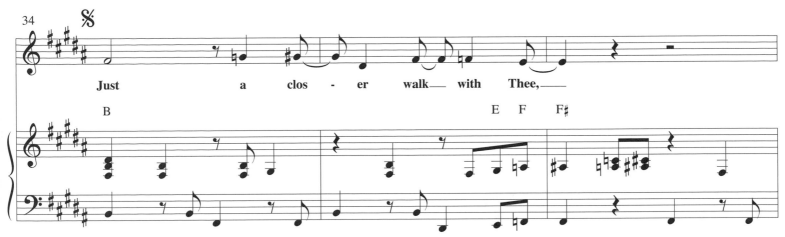

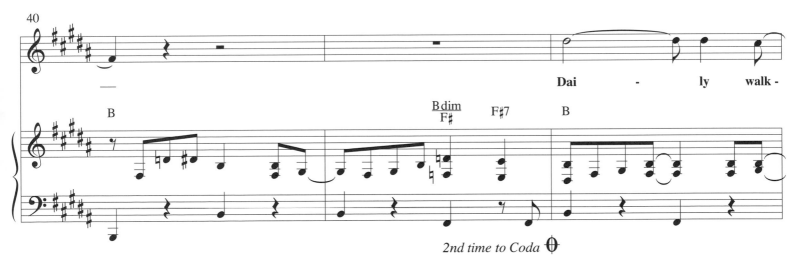

dear Lord,_____ let_____ it be,_____ yeah.

Vocal ad lib

Ooo Ooo Ooo_____

Ooo Ooo Yeah._____

(ad lib fill)

MawMaw's Song
(Sweet By And By)

**Words and Music by
BARRY GRAUL and
BART MILLARD**

times have changed— to say— the least. My Grand - ma - ma's voice a mem - o - ry.— Just

F   C   Dm   Am7

mf

like the old— song said,— she's on that shore.— And

B♭   F   C

if she's look - ing down— on me,— I hope— she's proud— of what— she sees,— 'cause

F   C   Dm   Am7

thanks to her— I'm a - walk - ing with— the Lord.—

B♭   F   C   C♯dim7

14

to pre - pare___ us___ a dwell - ing___ place___

Am · B♭ · C

___ there. · Oh,___ I can

B♭ · Gm · F · Gm/E · C

hear her___ sing - ing a - long.___ In the

B♭ · Gm · F · C7/E

sweet by___ and___ by we shall meet on___ that beau - ti - ful shore.___

F · C · Gm

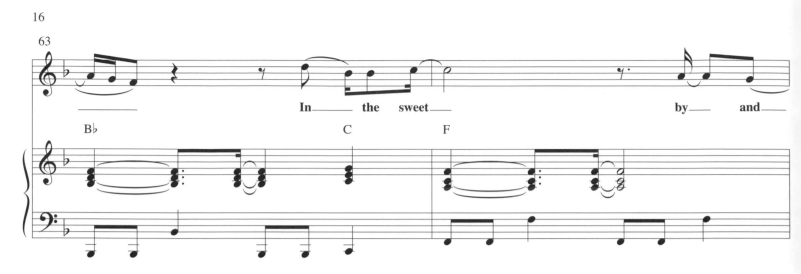

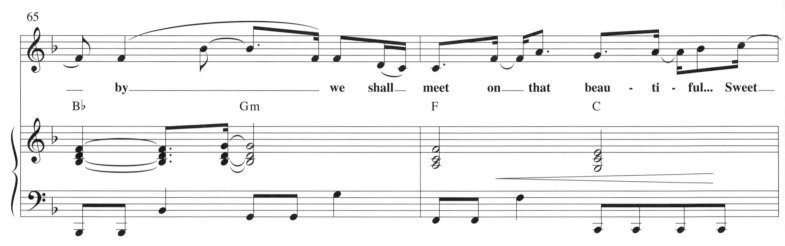

Pass Me Not, O Gentle Savior

Words by
FANNY J. CROSBY

Words and Music by
WILLIAM H. DOANE

1. Pass me not, O gentle Savior;
Hear my humble cry;

While_____ on oth - ers Thou___ art call - ing,___

A D A

Do_____ not pass me_____ by.___

E A

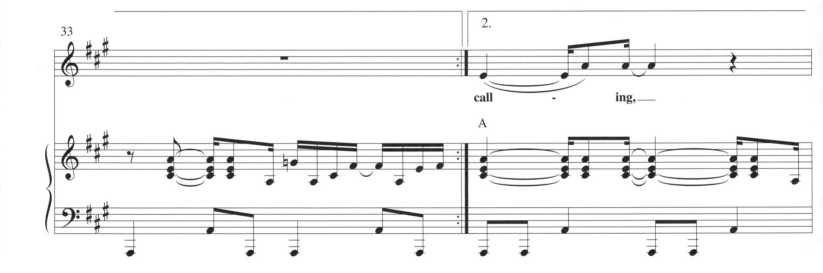

call - ing, —

Do — not pass — me — by. —

D.S. al CODA 𝄋

While_____ on oth - ers Thou__ art call - ing,_____

Lord,___ Do not pass me_____ by._____

Have A Little Talk With Jesus

Words and Music by
CLEAVANT DERRICKS

Precious Lord, Take My Hand

Words and Music by
THOMAS A. DORSEY

32

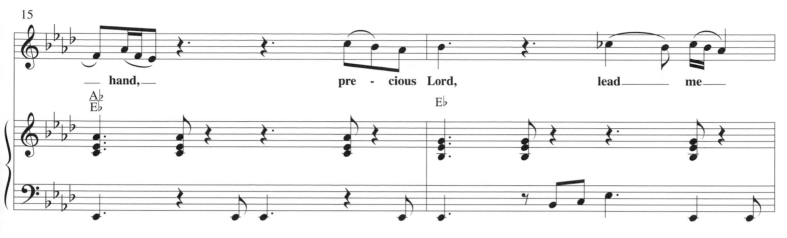

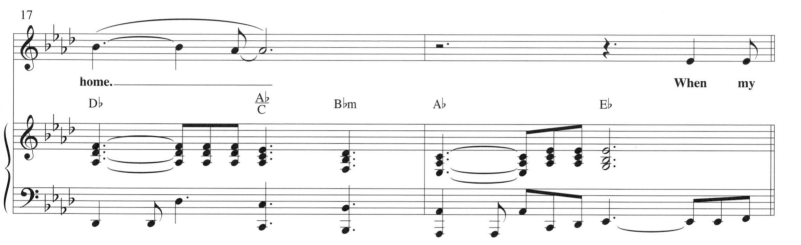

34

life, oh my life is al - most

Ab   Fm⁷

gone, woh, Hear my

Eb   Ebaug

cry, hear my call, Hold my

Ab   Ab7

hand lest I fall. Take my

Db   Ddim⁷

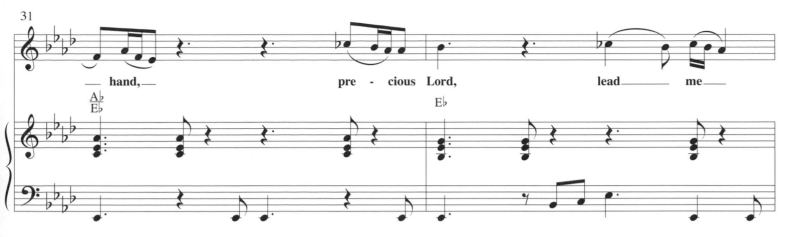

hand, pre - cious Lord, lead me

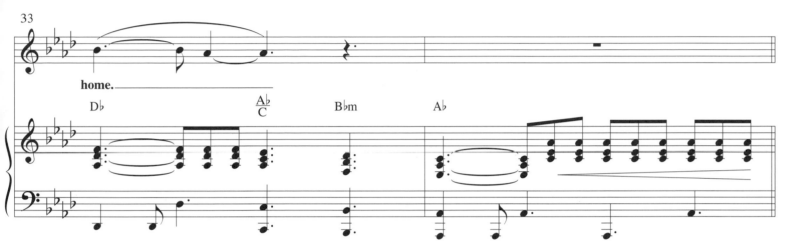

home.

Intstrumental

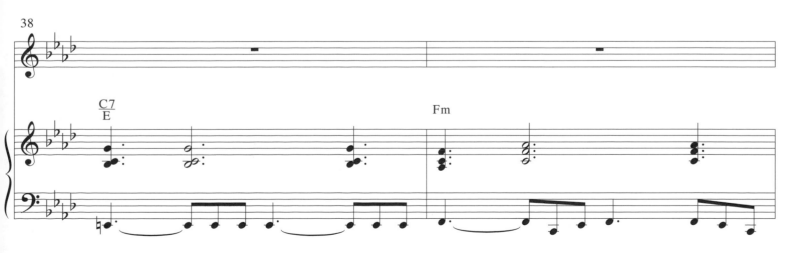

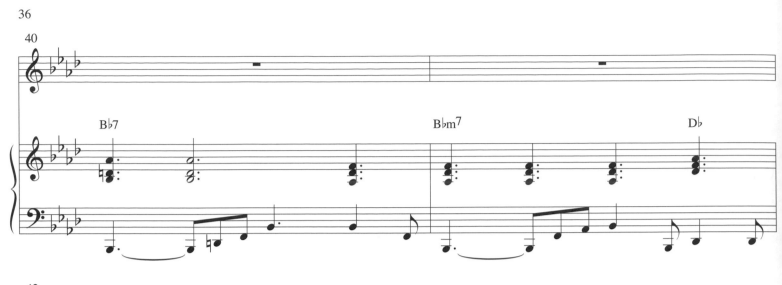

And_____ He walks_____ with me, and He

talks_____ with me,_____ And He tells me that I_____ am His

(ad lib freely to end)

own;_____ Oh, the joy we share_____ as we,

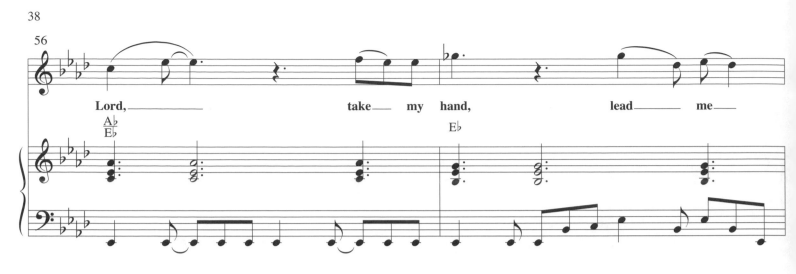

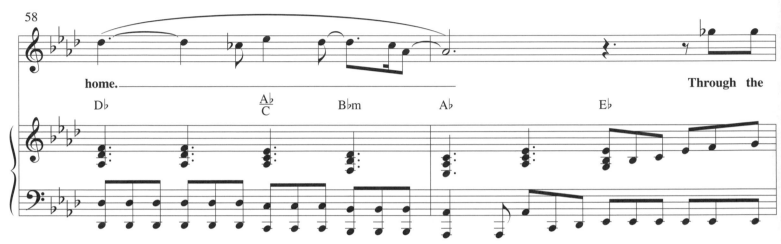

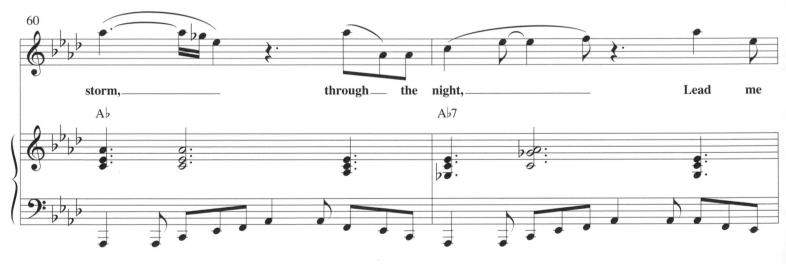

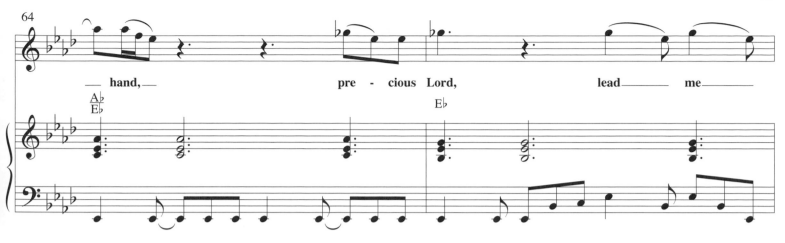

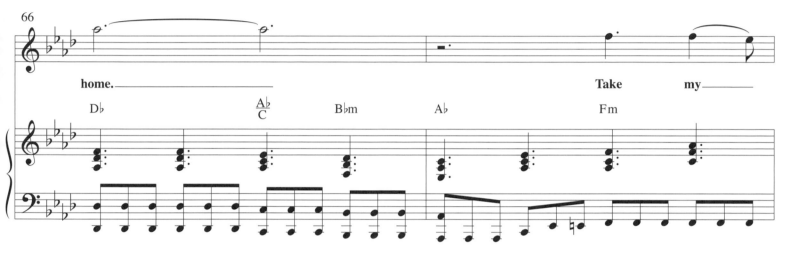

Softly And Tenderly

Words and Music by
WILL L. THOMPSON

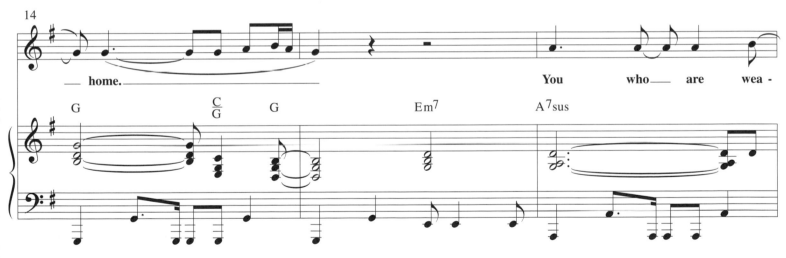

Ear - nest - ly, ten - der - ly Je - sus is call-

- ing, Call - ing, "O sin - ner, come

home!" Uh huh.

O for the won - der - ful love

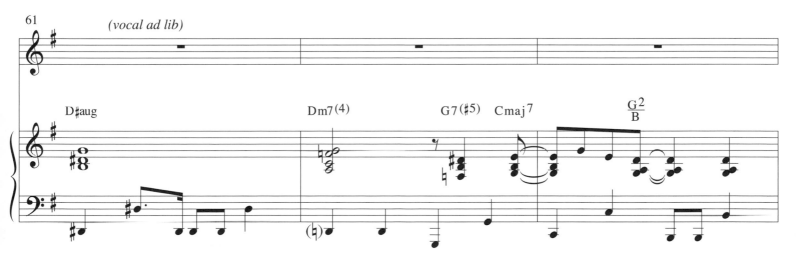

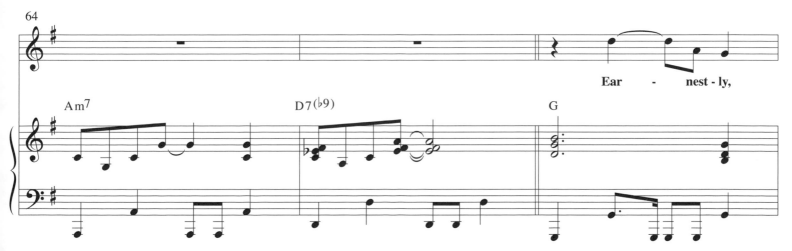

ten - der - ly___ Je - sus___ is call - ing,

Call - ing,___ "O___ sin - ner,___ come___

(ad lib freely on repeats)

(slide)

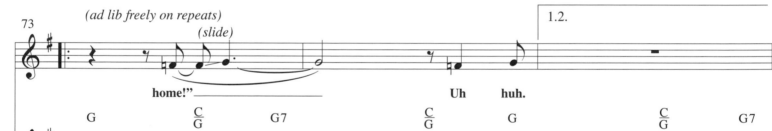

home!"_____ Uh huh.

1.2.

3.

It's time to come on home. Come___ on home.___

Sweetest Name I Know

Words and Music by
LUTHER B. BRIDGERS

With a groove ♩ = 102

There's with - in my heart_____ a mel - o - dy;_____

Je - sus whis - pers sweet_____ and low:_____

Traditional - Public Domain

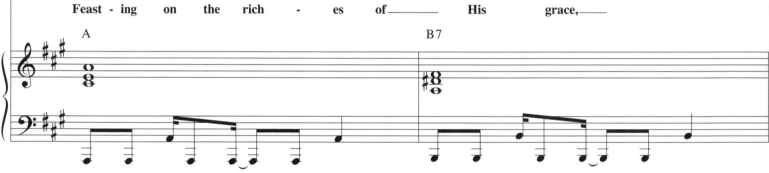

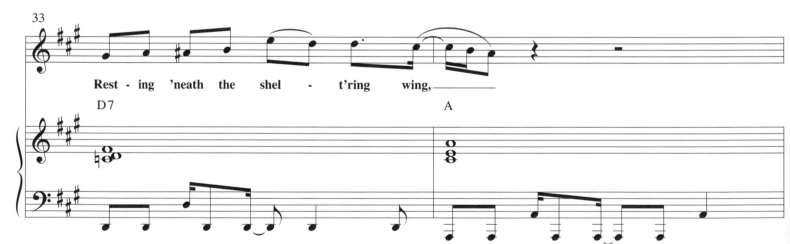

D.S. al CODA 𝄋

doot doot do do do.____

Doot do do doot____ doot do____ do do

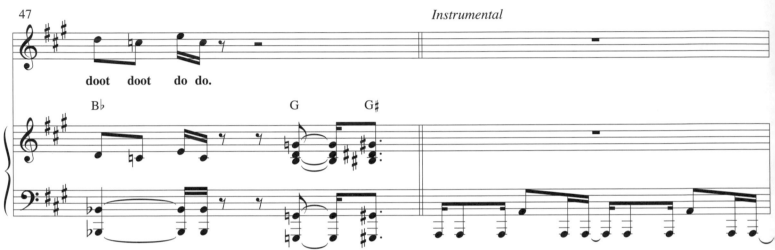

doot doot do do.

Instrumental

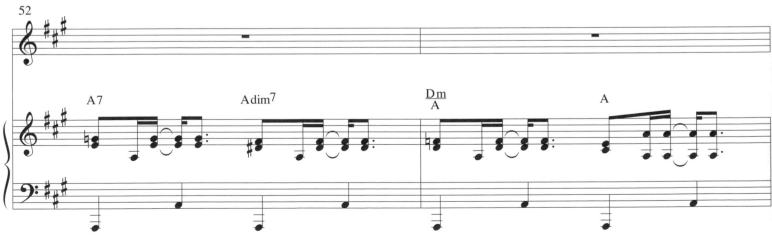

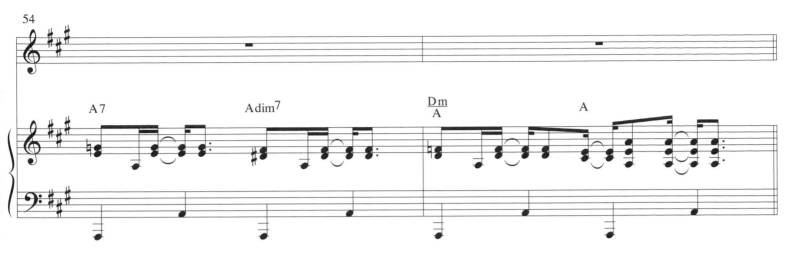

All my life was wrecked— by sin— and strife;— Dis - cord filled my heart— with pain.—

Je - sus swept a - cross— these

bro - ken strings,— and stirred these chords— a - gain.—

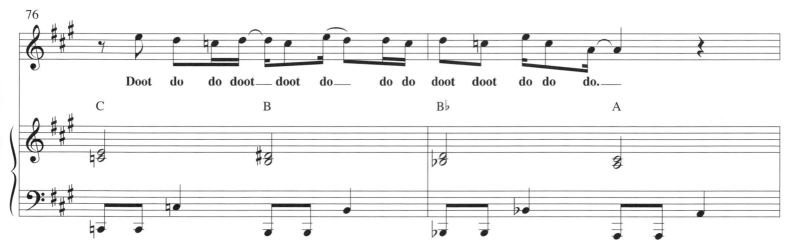

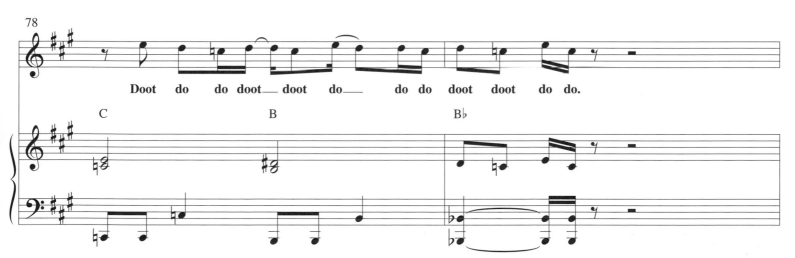

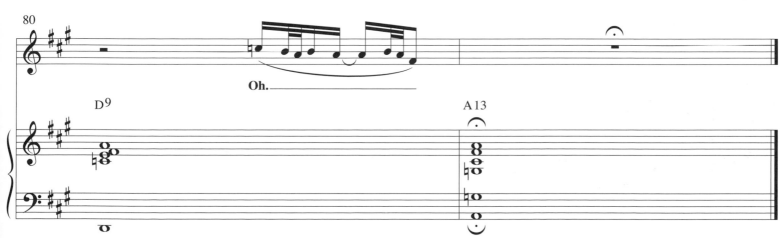

There Is Power In The Blood

**Words and Music by
LEWIS E. JONES**

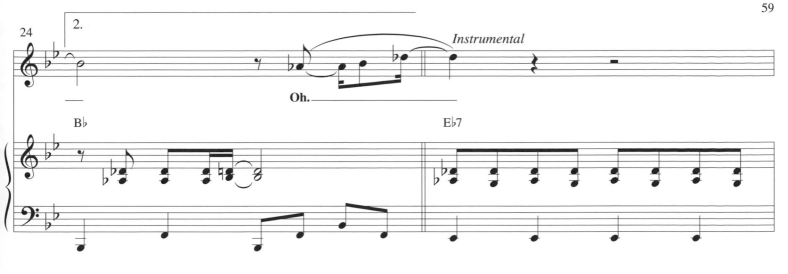

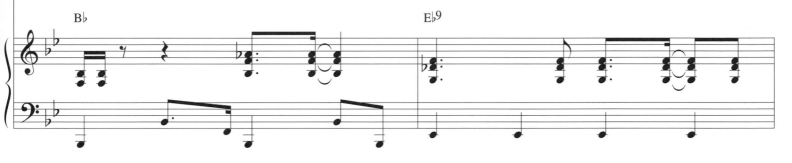

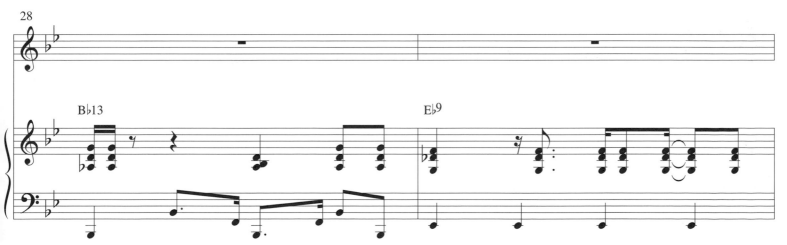

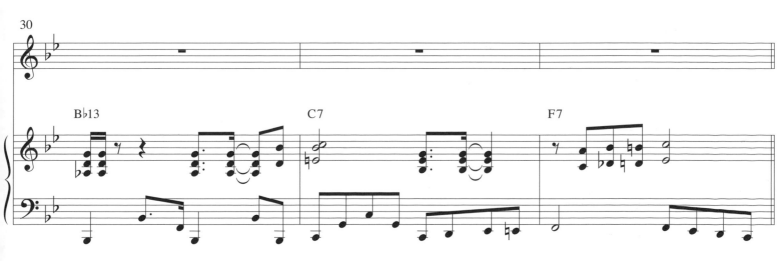

My Jesus, I Love Thee/'Tis So Sweet

Acoustic feel ♩ = 88

MY JESUS I LOVE THEE (Words: William Featherstone/Music: Adoniram J. Gordon)

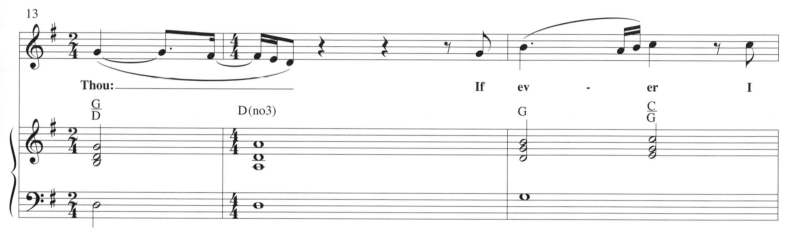

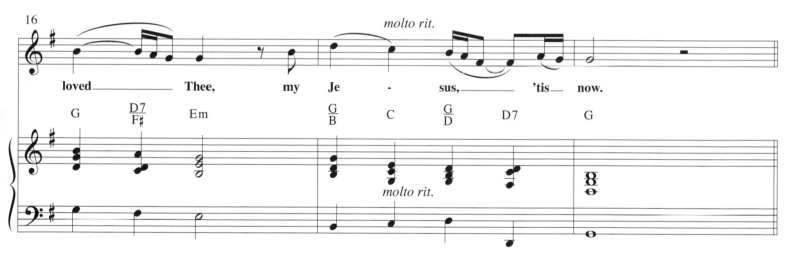

'TIS SO SWEET TO TRUST IN JESUS (Words: Louisa M. R. Stead/Music: William J. Kirkpatrick)

Traditional - Public Domain

29

Just to_____ rest up - on His
Just from_____ Je - sus sim - ply

G(no3)   C

31

prom - ise,   Just to_____ know: "Thus
tak - ing   Life and_____ rest,   and

G(no3)   C

33

saith the Lord."   Je - sus, Je - sus,_____
joy and peace.

G/D   D   G   G

36

how_____ I trust_____ Him! How I've proved_____ Him o'er_____ and o'er!_____

C   D   Em⁷   C

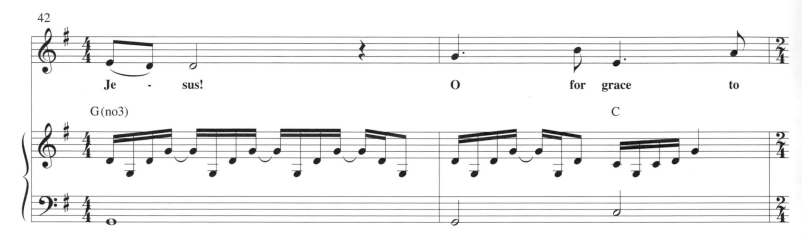

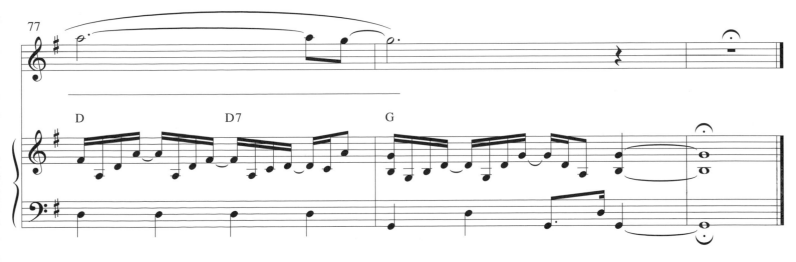

The Old Rugged Cross

Words and Music by
GEORGE BENNARD

sin - ners was_____ slain.
dark Cal - va - ry.

So I'll

cher - ish the old rug - ged cross,

Till my tro - phies at last I_____ lay_____

down.

I will cling to the

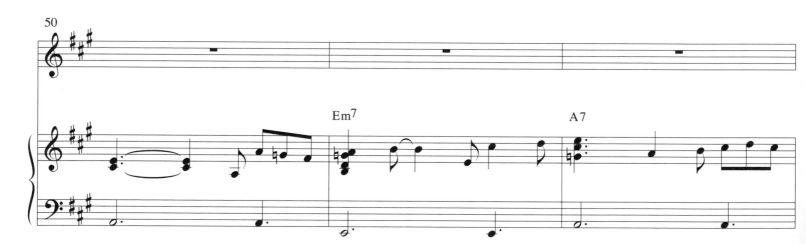

D.S. al CODA %

So— I'll

CODA

change——— it some - day   for   a——— crown,———

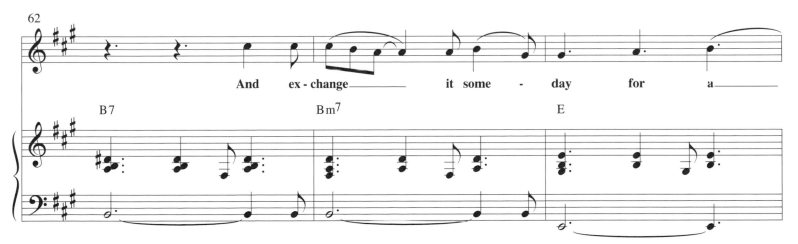

And ex - change———   it some - day   for   a———

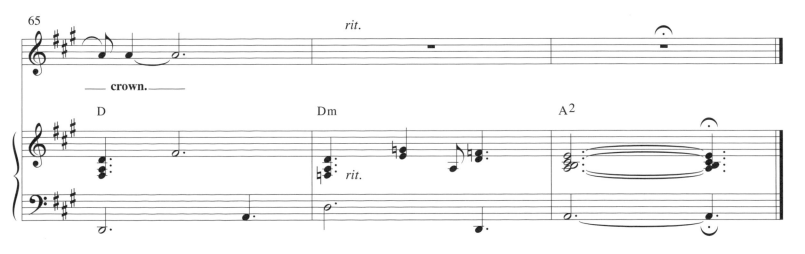

— crown.———